SCHOLASTIC

File-Folder Games in COLOR
Addition & Subtraction

by Immacula A. Rhodes

New York • Toronto • London • Auckland • Sydney
Mexico City • New Delhi • Hong Kong • Buenos Aires

Teaching Resources

To the many members of my large and loving family

"I know that everything God does will endure forever;
nothing can be added to it and nothing taken from it."

—Ecclesiastes 3:14

Cover and interior design by Jason Robinson
Cover and interior illustrations by Rusty Fletcher

ISBN-13: 978-0-545-22609-7

Text copyright © 2010 by Immacula A. Rhodes
Illustrations copyright © 2010 by Scholastic Inc.
Published by Scholastic Inc. All rights reserved.
Printed in China

1 2 3 4 5 6 7 8 9 10   16 15 14 13 12 11 10

Contents

File-Folder Games

About This Book

File-Folder Games in Color: Addition & Subtraction offers an engaging and fun way to motivate children of all learning styles and help them build skills in addition and subtraction. Research shows that attaining computational fluency is fundamental in developing more advanced math skills. In addition, the games in this book will help children meet important math standards. (See What the Research Says and Meeting the Math Standards, page 6, for more.)

The games are a snap to set up and store: Just pull out the full-color game boards from this book, glue them inside file folders, and you've got ten instant learning center activities. Children will have fun as they add to match squirrels to their tents in Camp Scamp-Along, solve addition facts to reach the treasure in Sums at Sea, subtract to fill in their turtle's shell in Turtle Toppers, find missing subtrahends to feed the bunnies in Breakfast for Bunnies, and much more.

What's Inside

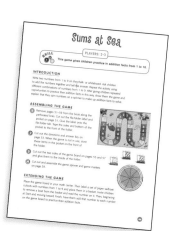

Each game includes the following:

- an introductory page for the teacher that provides suggestions for introducing the game

- step-by-step assembly directions

- Extending the Game activities to continue reinforcing children's skills and interest

- a label with the title of each game for the file-folder tab

- a pocket to attach to the front of the file folder for storing the game parts

- directions that explain to children how to play the game

- an answer key

- game cards

- one or more game boards

- some games also include game markers and a game cube, number pyramid, or spinner

Making the File-Folder Games

In addition to the game pages, you will need the following:

- 10 file folders (in a variety of colors, if possible)
- scissors
- clear packing tape
- glue stick or rubber cement
- paper clips
- brass fasteners

Tips

- Back the spinners, game cubes, number pyramids, and game markers with tagboard before assembling. Laminate for durability.
- Before cutting apart the game cards, make additional copies (in color or black and white) for use with the Extending the Game activities.
- Place the accessories for each game, such as spinners, game cubes, number pyramids, and game markers, in separate, labeled zipper storage bags. Keep the bags in a basket near the games.

Using the File-Folder Games

- Before introducing the games to children, conduct mini-lessons to review the addition and subtraction concepts used in each game.
- Model how to play each game. You might also play it with children the first time.
- Give children suggestions on how to determine the order in which players take turns, such as rolling a die and taking turns in numerical order.
- Store the games in a math center and encourage children to play in pairs or small groups before or after school, during free-choice time, or when they have finished other tasks.
- Send the games home for children to play with family members and friends.
- Use the Extending the Game activities to continue reinforcing children's skills and interest.

Storage Ideas

Keep the file-folder games in any of these places:

- math center
- vertical file tray
- file box
- file cabinet
- bookshelf
- plastic stacking crate

What the Research Says

Understanding how to use number and operations to solve problems is central to any mathematics curriculum. The National Council of Teachers of Mathematics (NCTM), in its *Principles and Standards for School Mathematics* (2000), stresses that knowing basic number combinations involving single-digit addition and subtraction pairs is essential. "Equally essential is computational fluency—having and using efficient and accurate methods for computing. . . . Computational fluency should develop in tandem with understanding of the role and meaning of arithmetic operations in number systems" (Hiebert et al. 1997; Thornton, 1990, as cited in *Principles and Standards of Mathematics*, 2000).

Meeting the Math Standards

Connections to the McREL Math Standards

Mid-continent Research for Education and Learning (McREL), a nationally recognized nonprofit organization, has compiled and evaluated national and state curriculum standards—and proposed what teachers should provide for their K–2 students to grow proficient in math, among other curriculum areas. The games and activities in this book support the following standards.

Uses a variety of strategies in the problem-solving process:

- Uses discussions with others to understand problems
- Explains how she or he went about solving a numerical problem

Understands and applies basic and advanced properties of the concepts of numbers:

- Understands that numerals are symbols used to represent quantities or attributes of real-world objects
- Understands symbolic, concrete, and pictorial representations of numbers
- Understands basic whole number relationships (for example, 4 is less than 10)

Uses basic and advanced procedures while performing the processes of computation:

- Adds and subtracts whole numbers
- Solves real-world problems involving addition and subtraction of whole numbers
- Understands the inverse relationship between addition and subtraction

Source: Kendall, J. S., & Marzano, R. J. (2004). *Content knowledge: A compendium of standards and benchmarks for K–12 education.* Aurora, CO: Mid-continent Research for Education and Learning. Online database: www.mcrel.org/standards-benchmarks

Connections to the NCTM Math Standards

The activities in this book are also designed to support you in meeting the following K–2 standards—including process standards, such as problem solving, reasoning and proof, and communication—recommended by the National Council of Teachers of Mathematics (NCTM).

Number and Operations

Understand meanings of operations and how they relate to one another

- Understand various meanings of addition and subtraction of whole numbers and the relationship between the two operations
- Understand the effects of adding and subtracting whole numbers
- Connect number words and numerals to the quantities they represent, using various physical models and representations

Compute fluently and make reasonable estimates

- Develop and use strategies for whole-number computations, with a focus on addition and subtraction
- Develop fluency with basic number combinations for addition and subtraction
- Use a variety of methods and tools to compute, including objects, mental computation, estimation, paper and pencil, and calculators

Source: National Council of Teachers of Mathematics. (2000). *Principles and standards for school mathematics.* Reston, VA: NCTM. www.nctm.org

Camp Scamp-Along

SKILL

This game gives children practice in addition facts with sums up to 10.

INTRODUCTION

Write the numbers 1–10 across the chalk- or whiteboard. Then show one game card at a time to children. Ask them to read the addition fact and tell the answer. Each time, invite a volunteer to find the answer on the board and write that math fact under it. Afterward, ask children if they can come up with other addition facts that equal each number on the board. Have them write the new facts under the corresponding sum.

ASSEMBLING THE GAME

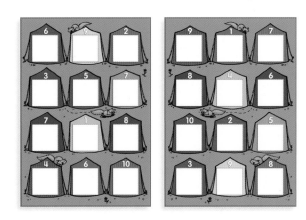

1. Remove pages 9–19 from the book along the perforated lines. Cut out the file-folder label and pocket on page 9. Glue the label onto the file-folder tab. Tape the sides and bottom of the pocket to the front of the folder.

2. Cut out the directions, answer key, and game cards on pages 11 and 13. When the game is not in use, store these items in the pocket on the front of the folder.

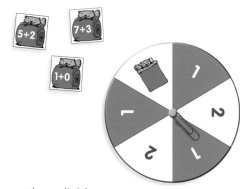

3. Cut out the two game boards on pages 15 and 17 and glue them to the inside of the folder.

4. Cut out and assemble the game spinner on page 19.

EXTENDING THE GAME

Write the answer for each game card on an acorn-shaped paper cutout. Then divide the class into two groups. Give one group the game cards and the other the acorns. Tell children they will pretend to be squirrels. On a signal, have the squirrels scamper to members of the other group, trying to match the problem and answer cards. Tell them that only one problem can be matched to each acorn. After finding all of the matches, invite children to share their findings with the class.

Camp Scamp-Along

PLAYERS: 2

GET READY TO PLAY

- Each player chooses a game board.
- Shuffle the cards. Stack them facedown.

TO PLAY

1 Spin the spinner. Take that number of cards.
If the spinner lands on the , your turn ends.

2 Solve the problem on each card and tell your answer.
Is that sum on one of your tents?
- If so, place the card on that tent.
- If not, place the card at the bottom of the stack.

3 After each turn, check the answer key. Is each answer correct?
If not, put that card at the bottom of the stack.

4 Keep taking turns. Try to cover all of your tents.
The first player to do this wins the game.

Camp Scamp-Along

ANSWER KEY

1: 0 + 1, 1 + 0

2: 1 + 1, 0 + 2

3: 1 + 2, 2 + 1

4: 3 + 1, 2 + 2

5: 4 + 1, 3 + 2

6: 3 + 3, 4 + 2, 5 + 1

7: 5 + 2, 6 + 1, 3 + 4

8: 7 + 1, 6 + 2, 5 + 3

9: 4 + 5, 7 + 2, 6 + 3

10: 7 + 3, 4 + 6

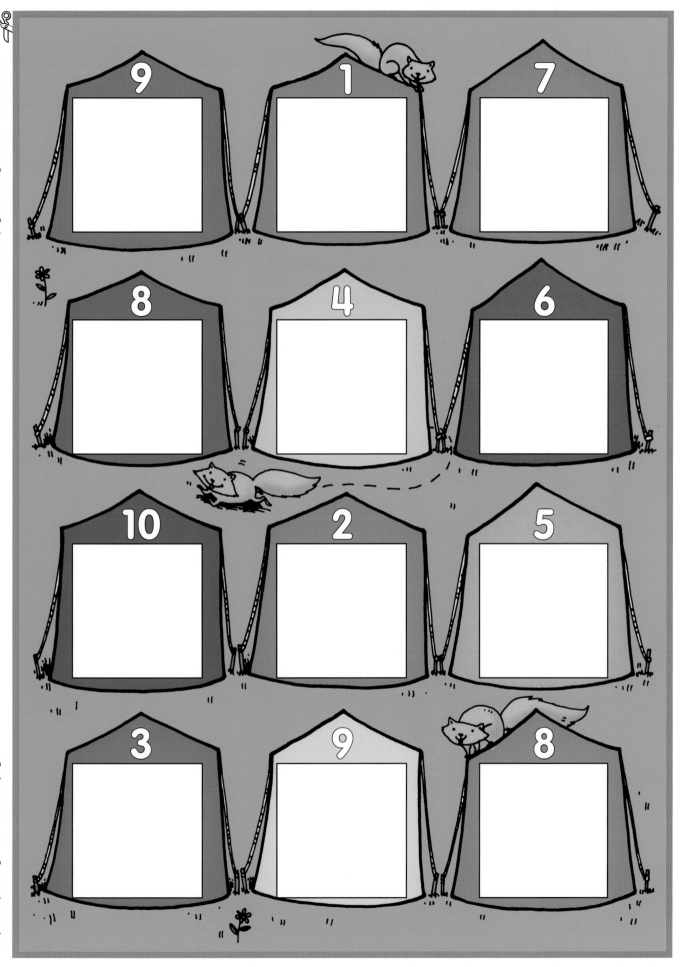

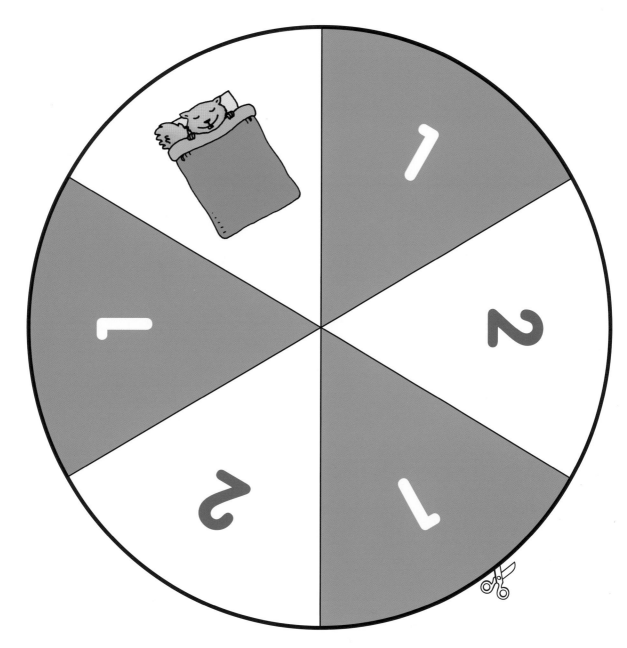

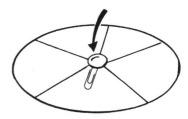

brass fastener

Assemble the spinner using a
paper clip and brass fastener as
shown. Make sure the paper clip
spins easily.

Hungry Caterpillars

SKILL

This game gives children practice in addition facts with sums from 11 to 18.

INTRODUCTION

Display the game boards. Point out that each caterpillar is missing its body. Show children the game cards, explaining that each card pictures a caterpillar body labeled with an addition fact. To match each body to the correct caterpillar, children will solve the addition fact and find a leaf that has that sum. Ask children to solve the problem on one game card at a time. Invite a volunteer to place each card on a leaf with the corresponding sum.

ASSEMBLING THE GAME

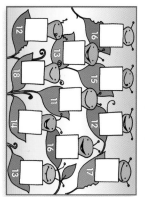
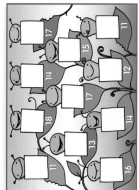

1. Remove pages 23–33 from the book along the perforated lines. Cut out the file-folder label and pocket on page 23. Glue the label onto the file-folder tab. Tape the sides and bottom of the pocket to the front of the folder.

2. Cut out the directions, answer key, and game cards on pages 25 and 27. When the game is not in use, store these items in the pocket on the front of the folder.

3. Cut out the two game boards on pages 29 and 31 and glue them to the inside of the folder.

4. Cut out and assemble the game cube on page 33.

EXTENDING THE GAME

Write addition facts that have sums from 11 to 18 on leaf-shaped paper cutouts. Create an eight-column chart. Label the headings with the numbers 11 to 18. Then, working with a small group, distribute the addition fact leaves to children. Have them solve each problem and place the leaf in the column labeled with the corresponding sum.

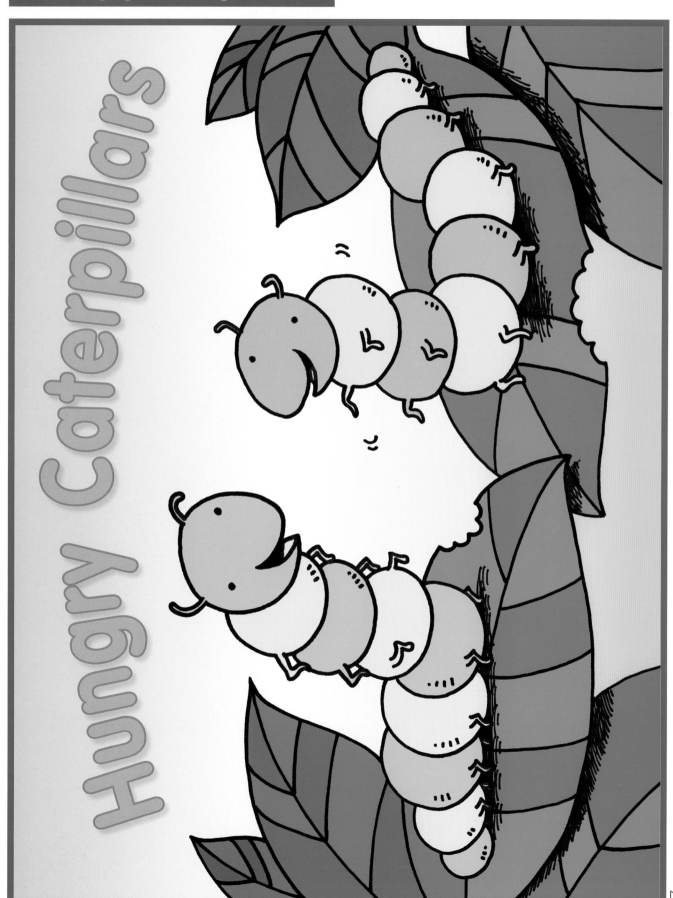

Hungry Caterpillars

PLAYERS: 2

GET READY TO PLAY

- Each player chooses a game board.
- Shuffle the cards. Stack them facedown.

TO PLAY

1 Roll the game cube. Take that number of cards.
If it lands on the , take one card.
Then roll again and take that number of cards.

2 Solve the problem on each card and tell your answer.
Is that sum on one of your leaves?
- If so, place the card on that leaf.
- If not, put the card at the bottom of the stack.

3 After each turn, check the answer key. Is each answer correct?
If not, put that card at the bottom of the stack.

4 Keep taking turns. Try to cover all of your boxes with caterpillar bodies.
The first player to do this wins the game.

PLAYING TIP

Players may place only one card on each of their boxes.

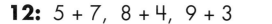

Hungry Caterpillars

ANSWER KEY

11: 5 + 6, 8 + 3, 9 + 2

12: 5 + 7, 8 + 4, 9 + 3

13: 7 + 6, 8 + 5, 9 + 4

14: 9 + 5, 6 + 8, 7 + 7

15: 7 + 8, 9 + 6

16: 9 + 7, 8 + 8, 10 + 6

17: 8 + 9, 9 + 8, 10 + 7

18: 9 + 9, 10 + 8

5 +6	8 +3	9 +2	5 +7
8 +4	9 +3	7 +6	8 +5
9 +4	9 +5	6 +8	7 +7
7 +8	9 +6	9 +7	8 +8
8 +9	9 +8	9 +9	10 +8
10 +7	10 +6		

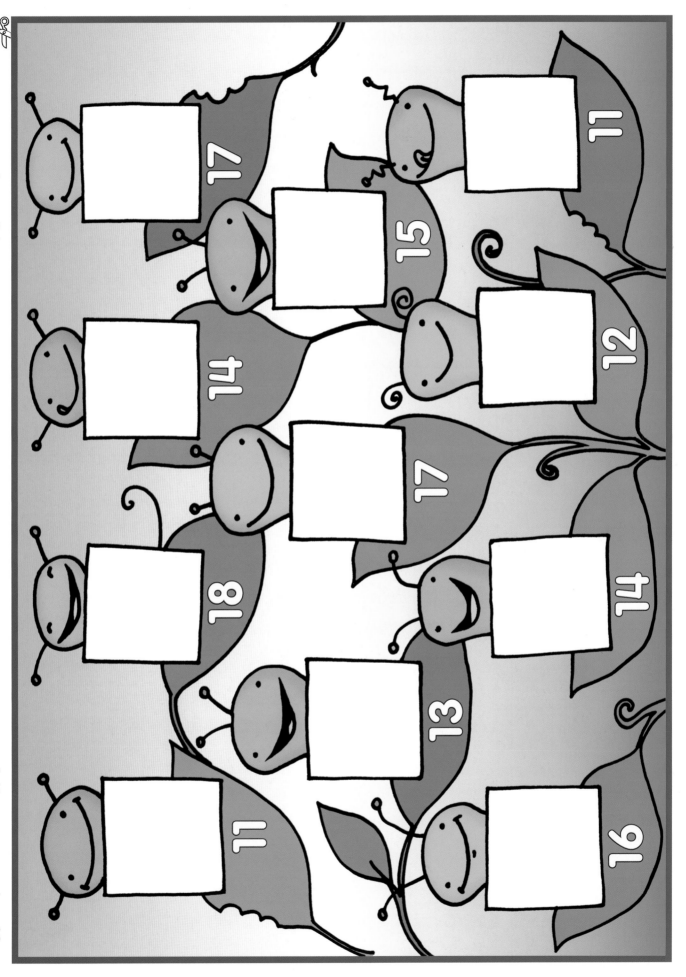

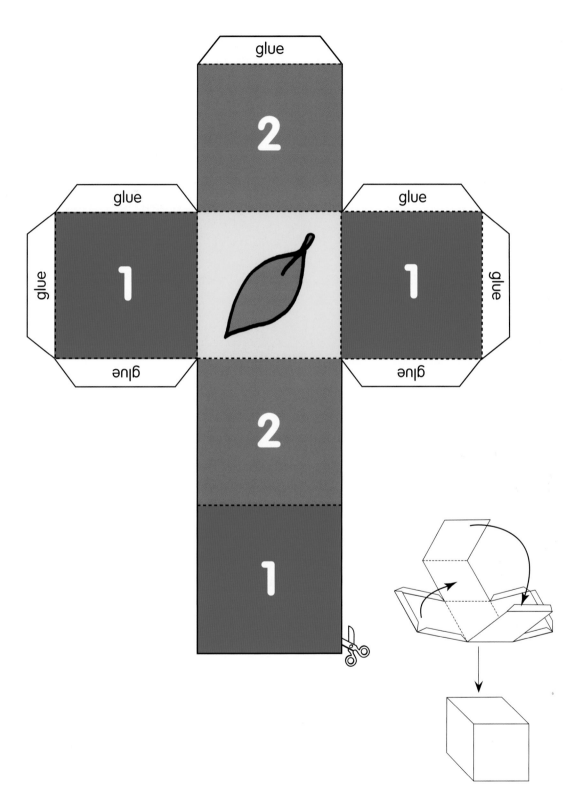

Assemble the cube by folding as shown. Glue closed.

Bubble Doubles

SKILL

This game gives children practice in adding identical addends with sums to 20.

INTRODUCTION

Display a game board. Then call out an addition fact that has identical addends (such as 2 + 2). Have children solve the problem and find the bubble labeled with the corresponding sum. Repeat, having children solve problems for identical addends from 1 to 10. Afterward, ask children to examine the numbers on the game board. Guide them to notice that all of them are even numbers. Explain that when two identical numbers are added together, the sum is always an even number.

ASSEMBLING THE GAME

1 Remove pages 37–47 from the book along the perforated lines. Cut out the file-folder label and pocket on page 37. Glue the label onto the file-folder tab. Tape the sides and bottom of the pocket to the front of the folder.

2 Cut out the directions, answer key, and game markers on pages 39 and 41. When the game is not in use, store these items in the pocket on the front of the folder.

3 Cut out the two game boards on pages 43 and 45 and glue them to the inside of the folder.

4 Cut out and assemble the game spinner on page 47.

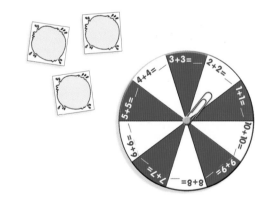

EXTENDING THE GAME

Draw a number line on the chalk- or whiteboard and label it with even numbers from 2 to 20. Then pass around the game spinner. Invite children to spin the spinner, read and solve the addition fact, and find the corresponding answer on the number line. If desired, you might have them write the problem under its sum on the number line.

Bubble Doubles

GET READY TO PLAY

Each player chooses a game board and ten ⬭ game markers.

TO PLAY

1 Spin the spinner. Solve the problem it lands on.

2 Is that sum on your game board?
- If so, "pop" that bubble by covering it with a ⬭.
- If not, or if that bubble is already covered, your turn ends.

3 After each turn, check the answer key. Is your answer correct? If not, take the ⬭ back.

4 Keep taking turns. Try to pop all of your bubbles. The first player to do this wins the game.

PLAYING TIP

Players may place only one game marker on each bubble on his or her game board.

Bubble Doubles

ANSWER KEY

2: 1 + 1

4: 2 + 2

6: 3 + 3

8: 4 + 4

10: 5 + 5

12: 6 + 6

14: 7 + 7

16: 8 + 8

18: 9 + 9

20: 10 + 10

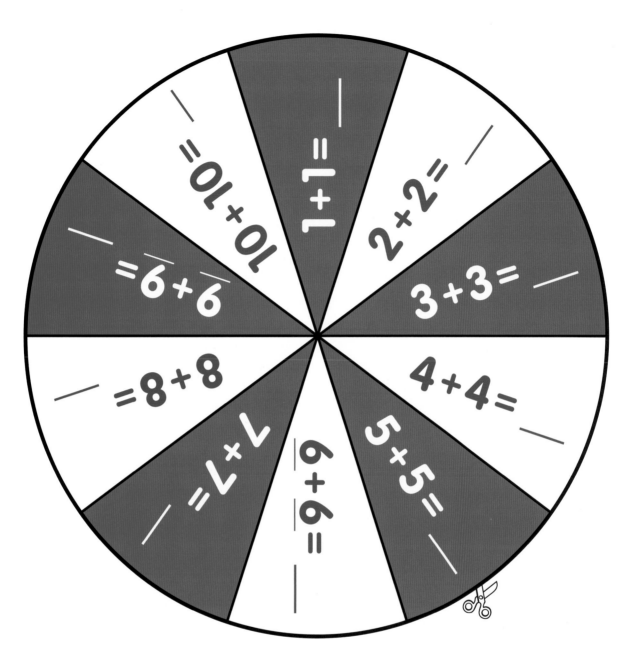

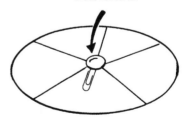

brass fastener

Assemble the spinner using a paper clip and brass fastener as shown. Make sure the paper clip spins easily.

Sums at Sea

 SKILL This game gives children practice in addition facts from 1 to 18.

INTRODUCTION

Write two numbers from 1 to 9 on the chalk- or whiteboard. Ask children to add the numbers together and tell the answer. Repeat the activity using different combinations of numbers from 1 to 9. After giving children repeated opportunities to practice their addition facts in this way, show them the game and explain that they spin numbers on a spinner to make up addition facts to solve.

ASSEMBLING THE GAME

1. Remove pages 51–59 from the book along the perforated lines. Cut out the file-folder label and pocket on page 51. Glue the label onto the file-folder tab. Tape the sides and bottom of the pocket to the front of the folder.

2. Cut out the directions and answer key on page 53. When the game is not in use, store these items in the pocket on the front of the folder.

3. Cut out the two sides of the game board on pages 55 and 57 and glue them to the inside of the folder.

4. Cut out and assemble the game spinner and game markers on page 59.

EXTENDING THE GAME

Place the game board in your math center. Then label a set of paper sailboat cutouts with numbers from 1 to 9 and place them in a basket. Invite children to remove a boat from the basket and read the number on it. Then, beginning at Start and moving toward Finish, have them add that number to each number on the game board to practice their addition facts.

Sums at Sea

GET READY TO PLAY

Each player puts a game marker on Start.

TO PLAY

1 Spin the spinner. Move that number of spaces.

2 What number does the spinner say to add?
Add that number to the number on the space.
Tell your answer.

3 Check the answer key. Is your answer correct?

- If so, leave your game marker on that space.
- If not, move your marker back to where it was.

4 Keep taking turns. The first player to reach Finish wins the game.

PLAYING TIP

Players may land on and share the same space.

Sums at Sea

ANSWER KEY

1 + 1 = 2	3 + 1 = 4	5 + 1 = 6	7 + 1 = 8	9 + 1 = 10
1 + 2 = 3	3 + 2 = 5	5 + 2 = 7	7 + 2 = 9	9 + 2 = 11
1 + 3 = 4	3 + 3 = 6	5 + 3 = 8	7 + 3 = 10	9 + 3 = 12
1 + 4 = 5	3 + 4 = 7	5 + 4 = 9	7 + 4 = 11	9 + 4 = 13
1 + 5 = 6	3 + 5 = 8	5 + 5 = 10	7 + 5 = 12	9 + 5 = 14
1 + 6 = 7	3 + 6 = 9	5 + 6 = 11	7 + 6 = 13	9 + 6 = 15
1 + 7 = 8	3 + 7 = 10	5 + 7 = 12	7 + 7 = 14	9 + 7 = 16
1 + 8 = 9	3 + 8 = 11	5 + 8 = 13	7 + 8 = 15	9 + 8 = 17
1 + 9 = 10	3 + 9 = 12	5 + 9 = 14	7 + 9 = 16	9 + 9 = 18
2 + 1 = 3	4 + 1 = 5	6 + 1 = 7	8 + 1 = 9	
2 + 2 = 4	4 + 2 = 6	6 + 2 = 8	8 + 2 = 10	
2 + 3 = 5	4 + 3 = 7	6 + 3 = 9	8 + 3 = 11	
2 + 4 = 6	4 + 4 = 8	6 + 4 = 10	8 + 4 = 12	
2 + 5 = 7	4 + 5 = 9	6 + 5 = 11	8 + 5 = 13	
2 + 6 = 8	4 + 6 = 10	6 + 6 = 12	8 + 6 = 14	
2 + 7 = 9	4 + 7 = 11	6 + 7 = 13	8 + 7 = 15	
2 + 8 = 10	4 + 8 = 12	6 + 8 = 14	8 + 8 = 16	
2 + 9 = 11	4 + 9 = 13	6 + 9 = 15	8 + 9 = 17	

Start

Cut along this edge and attach to page 57.

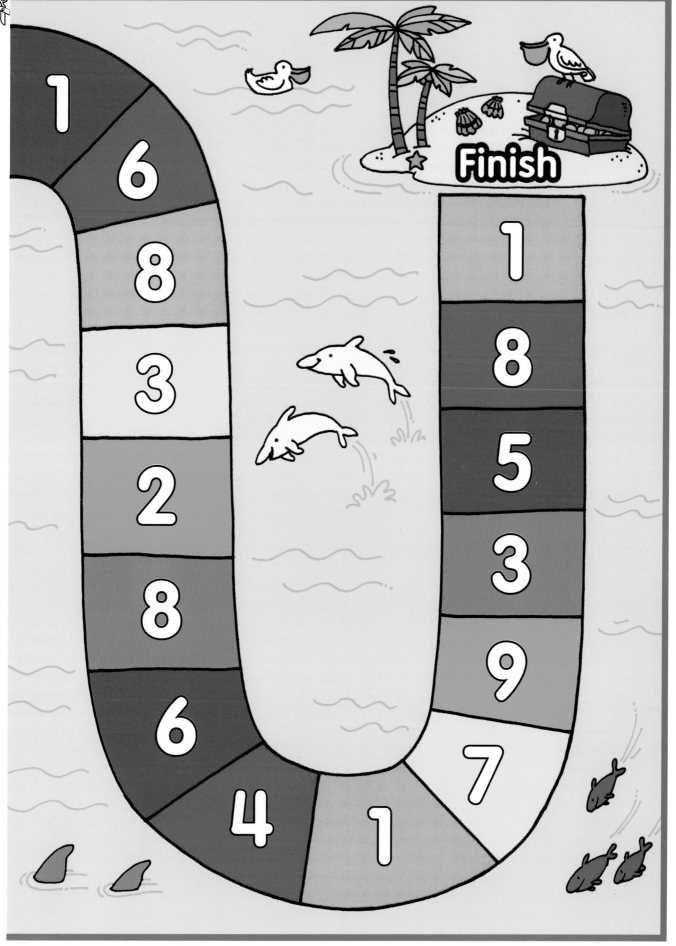

Finish

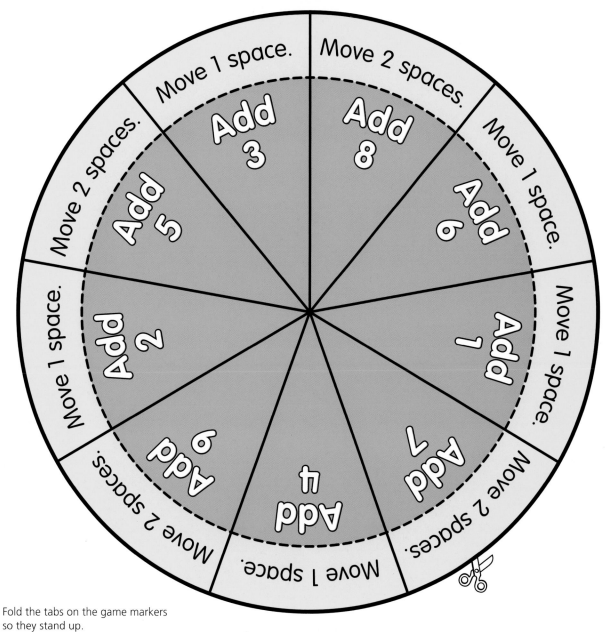

Fold the tabs on the game markers
so they stand up.

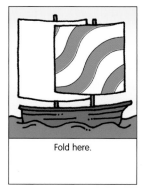

Fold here.

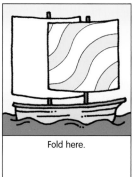

Fold here.

Fold here.

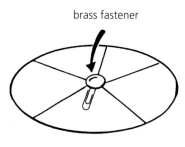

brass fastener

Assemble the spinner using a
paper clip and brass fastener as
shown. Make sure the paper clip
spins easily.

Pelican's Picnic

SKILL

This game gives children practice in finding missing addends.

INTRODUCTION

Show children one of the game cards. Explain that the blank line in the equation means that a number—one of the addends—is missing. Work with children to find the missing number. Then repeat, using one game card at a time. As children solve each problem, invite volunteers to share their strategies for discovering the missing addend.

ASSEMBLING THE GAME

1 Remove pages 63–73 from the book along the perforated lines. Cut out the file-folder label and pocket on page 63. Glue the label onto the file-folder tab. Tape the sides and bottom of the pocket to the front of the folder.

2 Cut out the directions, answer key, and game cards on pages 65 and 67. When the game is not in use, store these items in the pocket on the front of the folder.

3 Cut out the two game boards on pages 69 and 71 and glue them to the inside of the folder.

4 Cut out and assemble the number pyramid on page 73.

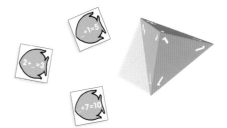

EXTENDING THE GAME

Copy one game board and the game cards. Cut out the boxes from the game board, then laminate them and the game cards. Pair up each number card from 1 to 9 with a game card in which each number is used to complete the equation. Invite children to use the card pairs to play Memory. On each turn, they try to find a problem card and the corresponding card labeled with the number that can be used to solve the problem.

Pelican's Picnic

GET READY TO PLAY

- Each player chooses a game board.
- Shuffle the cards. Stack them facedown.

TO PLAY

1 Roll the number pyramid. Take that number of cards.

2 Read the problem on each card. Tell what number goes in the blank to solve the problem. Is that number on your game board?

- If so, place the card on that box.
- If not, put the card at the bottom of the stack.

3 After each turn, check the answer key. Is each answer correct? If not, put that card on the bottom of the stack.

4 Keep taking turns. Try to cover all of your boxes. The first player to do this wins the game.

PLAYING TIP

Players may place only one card on each box on their game board.

Pelican's Picnic

ANSWER KEY

1: 2 + <u>1</u> = 3,   <u>1</u> + 1 = 2

2: <u>2</u> + 2 = 4,   3 + <u>2</u> = 5

3: 6 + <u>3</u> = 9,   <u>3</u> + 7 = 10,   8 + <u>3</u> = 11

4: <u>4</u> + 1 = 5,   <u>4</u> + 5 = 9,   9 + <u>4</u> = 13

5: <u>5</u> + 2 = 7,   6 + <u>5</u> = 11

6: 9 + <u>6</u> = 15,   <u>6</u> + 2 = 8,   1 + <u>6</u> = 7

7: 3 + <u>7</u> = 10,   <u>7</u> + 1 = 8,   8 + <u>7</u> = 15

8: 3 + <u>8</u> = 11,   <u>8</u> + 9 = 17,   4 + <u>8</u> = 12

9: <u>9</u> + 3 = 12,   5 + <u>9</u> = 14,   <u>9</u> + 7 = 16

2+_=3	_+1=2	_+2=4	3+_=5
6+_=9	_+7=10	8+_=11	_+1=5
_+5=9	9+_=13	_+2=7	6+_=11
9+_=15	_+2=8	1+_=7	3+_=10
_+1=8	8+_=15	3+_=11	_+9=17
4+_=12	_+3=12	5+_=14	_+7=16

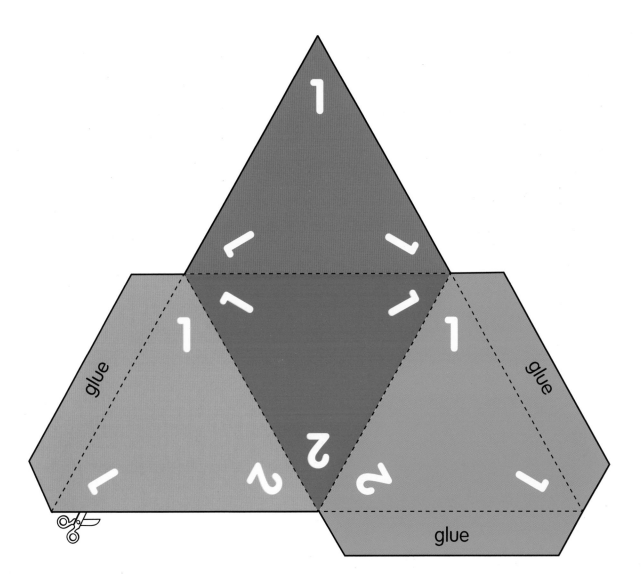

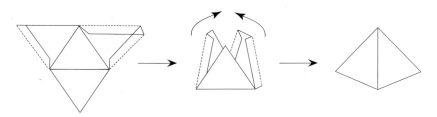

Assemble the pyramid by folding as shown. Glue closed.

Crocodile Smile

SKILL

This game gives children practice in subtraction facts with differences from 1 to 10.

INTRODUCTION

Draw a number line on the chalk- or whiteboard using the numbers 1–10. Show one of the game cards to children and read the problem aloud. Demonstrate how to use the number line to find the answer to the problem. Then show children each of the remaining game cards—one at a time. Ask them to read the subtraction fact and tell the answer, using the number line as needed to help them find the answer.

ASSEMBLING THE GAME

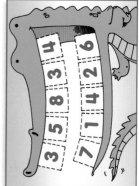

1. Remove pages 77–87 from the book along the perforated lines. Cut out the file-folder label and pocket on page 77. Glue the label onto the file-folder tab. Tape the sides and bottom of the pocket to the front of the folder.

2. Cut out the directions, answer key, teeth markers, and game cards on pages 79, 81, and 87. When the game is not in use, store these items in the pocket on the front of the folder.

3. Cut out the two game boards on pages 83 and 85 and glue them to the inside of the folder.

4. Cut out and assemble the game spinner on page 87.

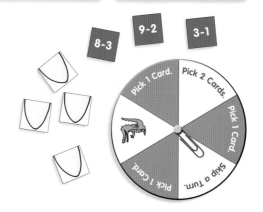

EXTENDING THE GAME

Invite children to play Snap! First, distribute the cards evenly between two children. Ask them to stack their cards facedown in front of them. Then have both children turn over the top card in their stack, solve the problem, and tell the answer. The child with the highest answer calls out "Snap!" and snaps up the two cards to set aside. If the cards are a tie, children play a tie-breaker round and the winner takes all the cards from that round. The player with the most cards at the end of the game is the winner.

Crocodile Smile

PLAYERS: 2

GET READY TO PLAY

- Each player chooses a game board and ten ⋃ game markers.
- Shuffle the cards. Stack them facedown.

TO PLAY

1 Spin the spinner. Take that number of cards. If it lands on the 🐊, take one card. Then spin again and take that number of cards.

2 Solve the problem on each card and tell your answer. Is that number on your game board?
- If so, place a ⋃ on that box. Keep the card.
- If not, place the card at the bottom of the stack.

3 After each turn, check the answer key. Is each answer correct? If not, take that ⋃ back.

4 Keep taking turns. Try to cover all of your boxes. The first player to do this wins the game.

PLAYING TIP

Players may place only one ⋃ on each box on their game board.

Crocodile Smile

ANSWER KEY

1: 2 – 1,   4 – 3,   5 – 4,   6 – 5   **6:** 8 – 2,   9 – 3

2: 3 – 1,   9 – 7,   10 – 8   **7:** 9 – 2,   10 – 3

3: 5 – 2,   7 – 4,   8 – 5   **8:** 9 – 1,   10 – 2

4: 6 – 2,   9 – 5,   10 – 6   **9:** 10 – 1

5: 7 – 2,   8 – 3,   9 – 4,   10 – 5

2-1	3-1	5-2	6-2	7-2
8-2	9-2	9-1	10-1	4-3
9-7	7-4	9-5	8-3	9-3
10-3	10-2	5-4	10-8	8-5

More cards on page 87.

Pick 1 Card.

Pick 2 Cards.

Pick 1 Card.

Skip a Turn.

Pick 1 Card.

10-5

10-6 9-4 6-5

brass fastener

Assemble the spinner using a paper clip and brass fastener as shown. Make sure the paper clip spins easily.

Strawberry Patch

PLAYERS: 2-3

SKILL

This game gives children practice in subtraction facts with differences from 11 to 18.

INTRODUCTION

Write the numbers 1 to 9 in a horizontal line on the chalk- or whiteboard. Then show one game card at a time to children. Read the subtraction fact and have them solve the problem. Then invite a volunteer to attach the card to the board under the corresponding number using removable adhesive. After using all of the game cards, ask children to come up with other subtraction problems that use 11 to 18 as the minuend (the first number in the equation) and have differences from 1 to 9. Have them write their problems under the corresponding number on the board.

ASSEMBLING THE GAME

1 Remove pages 91–101 from the book along the perforated lines. Cut out the file-folder label and pocket on page 91. Glue the label onto the file-folder tab. Tape the sides and bottom of the pocket to the front of the folder.

2 Cut out the directions, answer key, and game cards on pages 93 and 95. When the game is not in use, store these items in the pocket on the front of the folder.

3 Cut out the two sides of the game board on pages 97 and 99 and glue them to the inside of the folder.

4 Cut out and assemble the game cube and game markers on page 101.

EXTENDING THE GAME

Cut out nine strawberry shapes from red paper. Label each shape with a number from 1 to 9. Put the number cards in a center with the game cards. To use, ask children to line up the strawberries in numerical order. Then have them solve the problem on each card and place it with the strawberry labeled with that answer.

Strawberry Patch

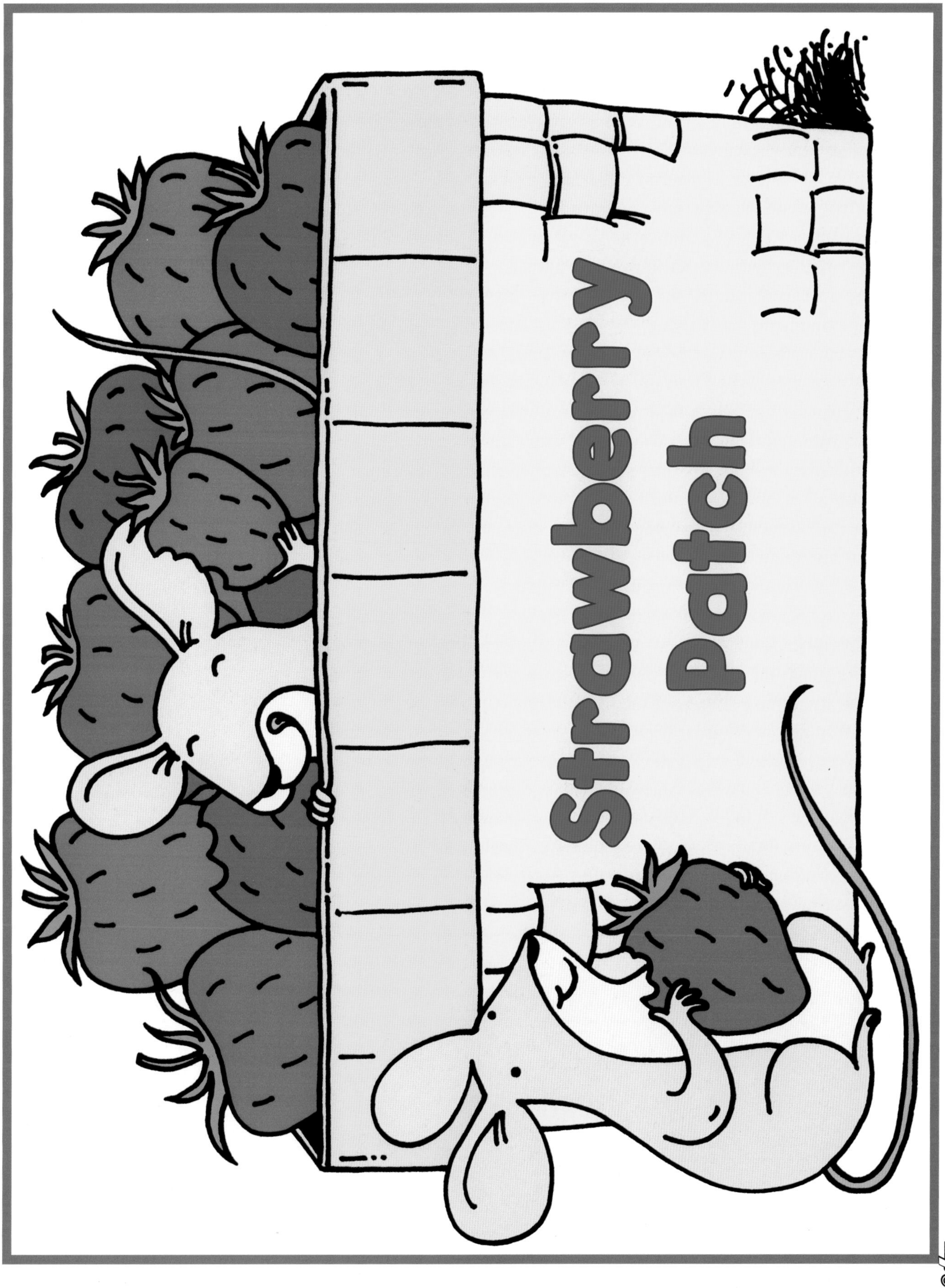

Strawberry Patch

PLAYERS: 2-3

GET READY TO PLAY

- Each player chooses a game marker. Place each marker on Start.

- Shuffle the game cards. Stack them facedown on the game board.

TO PLAY

1 Roll the game cube. Take that number of cards.
If it lands on the 🍓, your turn ends.

2 Did you pick one card? If so, solve the problem
and tell your answer. Then check the answer key.
Is your answer correct?

- If so, move your marker ahead to the closest space with that number.

- If not, your turn ends.

3 Do you have another card? If so, repeat step 2.

4 At the end of your turn, put each game card at the bottom of the stack.

5 Keep taking turns. The first player to reach Finish wins the game.

PLAYING TIP

Players may land on and share the same space.

Strawberry Patch

ANSWER KEY

1: 11 – 10

2: 11 – 9

3: 12 – 9,   11 – 8

4: 12 – 8,   11 – 7

5: 14 – 9,   13 – 8,   12 – 7

6: 15 – 9,   14 – 8,   13 – 7,   11 – 5

7: 16 – 9,   14 – 7,   13 – 6,   12 – 5

8: 17 – 9,   15 – 7,   13 – 5,   11 – 3

9: 18 – 9,   16 – 7,   13 – 4

Cut along this edge and attach to page 99.

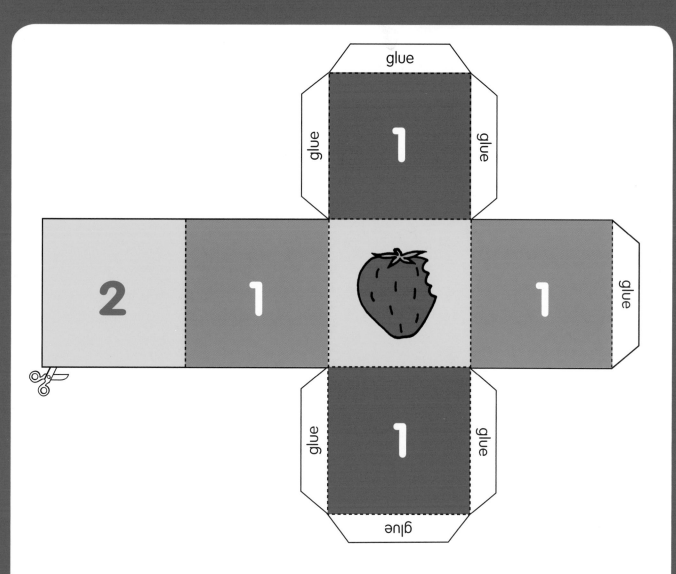

Fold the tabs on the game markers
so they stand up.

Fold here.

Fold here.

Fold here.

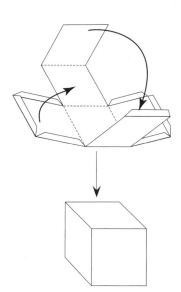

Assemble the cube by folding as shown. Glue closed.

Turtle Toppers

 SKILL

This game gives children practice in subtraction facts with differences from 0 to 18.

INTRODUCTION

Display copies of the game boards. Then show one game card at a time to children. Ask them to solve the subtraction problem and find that number on a turtle. Invite a volunteer to attach the game card to that box on one of the turtles using tape. Point out that the design on the game card resembles a design found on a turtle's shell. Then have children continue solving the problems and attaching them to the turtles until they have covered all the boxes on the turtles.

ASSEMBLING THE GAME

 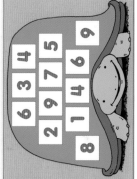

1 Remove pages 105–115 from the book along the perforated lines. Cut out the file-folder label and pocket on page 105. Glue the label onto the file-folder tab. Tape the sides and bottom of the pocket to the front of the folder.

2 Cut out the directions, answer key, and game cards on pages 107 and 109. When the game is not in use, store these items in the pocket on the front of the folder.

3 Cut out the two game boards on pages 111 and 113 and glue them to the inside of the folder.

4 Cut out and assemble the game cube on page 115.

EXTENDING THE GAME

Draw a 20-dot number line on a sentence strip, spacing the dots about an inch apart. Have each of two children place a button "turtle" next to the 1 on the number-line "race track." Then shuffle and stack the game cards facedown. To use, children take turns picking the top card, solving the problem, and moving their turtle that number of spaces along the number line. The first turtle to reach 20 wins the race!

Turtle Toppers

GET READY TO PLAY

- Each player chooses a game board.
- Shuffle the cards. Stack them facedown.

TO PLAY

1 Roll the game cube. Take that number of cards.
If it lands on the 🐢, your turn ends.

2 Solve the problem on each card. Is that number on your turtle?
- If so, place the card on a box with that number.
- If not, put the card at the bottom of the stack.

3 After each turn, check the answer key. Is each answer correct?
If not, put that card at the bottom of the stack.

4 Keep taking turns. Try to cover all of your boxes.
The first player to do this wins the game.

Turtle Toppers

ANSWER KEY

1: 3 – 2,   8 – 7

2: 6 – 4,   7 – 5   **6:** 7 – 1,   9 – 3,   13 – 7

3: 9 – 6,   10 – 7   **7:** 8 – 1,   11 – 4,   15 – 8

4: 5 – 1,   7 – 3,   8 – 4   **8:** 12 – 4,   14 – 6,   16 – 8

5: 6 – 1,   11 – 6,   14 – 9   **9:** 12 – 3,   15 – 6,   18 – 9

3-2	8-7	6-4	7-5
9-6	10-7	5-1	7-3
8-4	6-1	11-6	14-9
7-1	9-3	13-7	8-1
11-4	15-8	12-4	14-6
16-8	12-3	15-6	18-9

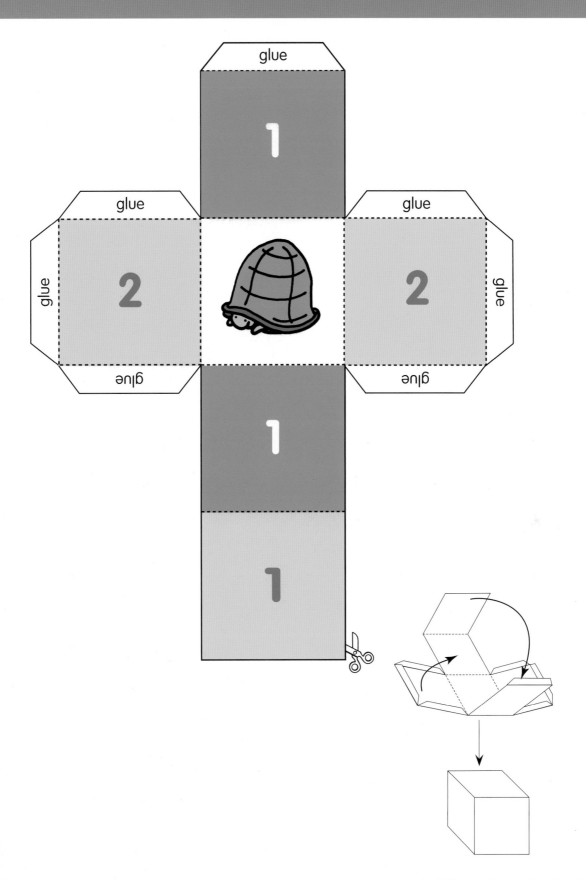

glue

1

glue glue glue

2 2

glue glue

1

1

Assemble the cube by folding as shown. Glue closed.

Breakfast for Bunnies

SKILL

This game gives children practice in solving subtraction problems with missing subtrahends.

INTRODUCTION

Show children one of the game cards. Explain that the blank line in the equation means that a number—the subtrahend—is missing. Work with children to find the missing number. Then repeat, using one game card at a time. As children solve each problem, invite volunteers to share their strategies for discovering the missing number.

ASSEMBLING THE GAME

1. Remove pages 119–129 from the book along the perforated lines. Cut out the file-folder label and pocket on page 119. Glue the label onto the file-folder tab. Tape the sides and bottom of the pocket to the front of the folder.

2. Cut out the directions, answer key, and game cards on pages 121 and 123. When the game is not in use, store these items in the pocket on the front of the folder.

3. Cut out the game boards on pages 125 and 127 and glue them to the inside of the folder.

4. Cut out and assemble the number pyramid on page 129.

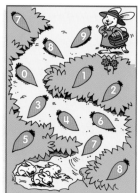

EXTENDING THE GAME

Write the answer for each game card on a carrot-shaped paper cutout. Then divide the class into two groups. Give one group the game cards and the other the carrots. Tell children they will pretend to be bunnies. On a signal, have the bunnies hop to members of the other group, trying to match the problem and answer cards. Tell them that only one problem can be matched to each carrot. After finding all of the matches, invite children to share their findings with the class.

Breakfast for Bunnies

GET READY TO PLAY

- Each player chooses a game board.
- Shuffle the cards. Stack them facedown.

TO PLAY

1 Roll the number pyramid. Take that number of cards.

2 Read the problem on each card. Tell what number goes in the blank to solve the problem. Is that number on a 🥕 on your game board?
- If so, place the card on the 🥕.
- If not, put the card at the bottom of the stack.

3 After each turn, check the answer key. Is each answer correct? If not, put that card at the bottom of the stack.

4 Keep taking turns. Try to cover each 🥕 on the path to the bunnies. The first player to do this wins the game.

PLAYING TIP

Players may place only one card on each 🥕 on their game board.

Breakfast for Bunnies

ANSWER KEY

0: $4 - \underline{0} = 4$

1: $10 - \underline{1} = 9$, $7 - \underline{1} = 6$

2: $7 - \underline{2} = 5$, $5 - \underline{2} = 3$

3: $9 - \underline{3} = 6$, $4 - \underline{3} = 1$

4: $7 - \underline{4} = 3$, $11 - \underline{4} = 7$

5: $12 - \underline{5} = 7$, $9 - \underline{5} = 4$, $6 - \underline{5} = 1$

6: $14 - \underline{6} = 8$, $11 - \underline{6} = 5$, $8 - \underline{6} = 2$

7: $15 - \underline{7} = 8$, $10 - \underline{7} = 3$, $9 - \underline{7} = 2$

8: $17 - \underline{8} = 9$, $14 - \underline{8} = 6$, $13 - \underline{8} = 5$

9: $17 - \underline{9} = 8$, $15 - \underline{9} = 6$, $12 - \underline{9} = 3$

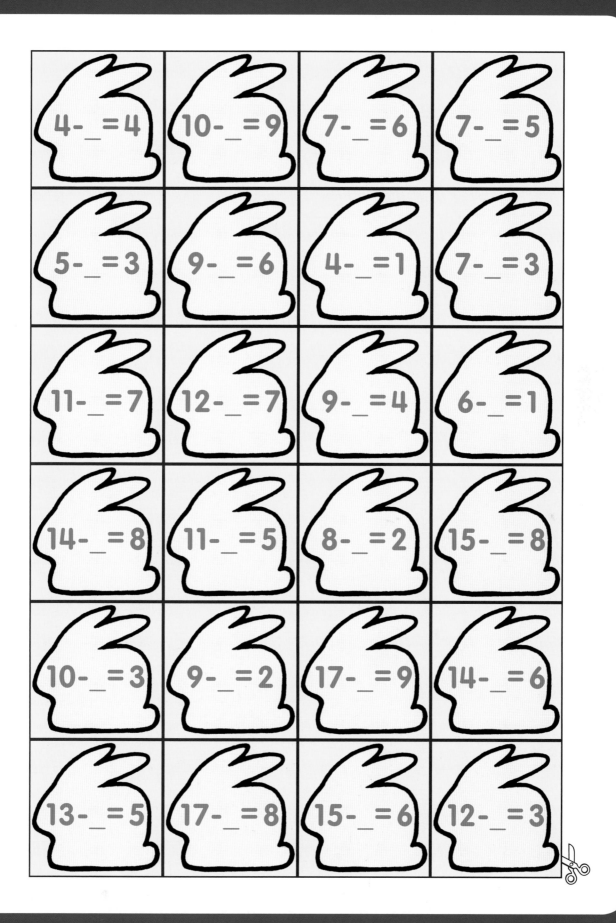

4-_=4	10-_=9	7-_=6	7-_=5
5-_=3	9-_=6	4-_=1	7-_=3
11-_=7	12-_=7	9-_=4	6-_=1
14-_=8	11-_=5	8-_=2	15-_=8
10-_=3	9-_=2	17-_=9	14-_=6
13-_=5	17-_=8	15-_=6	12-_=3

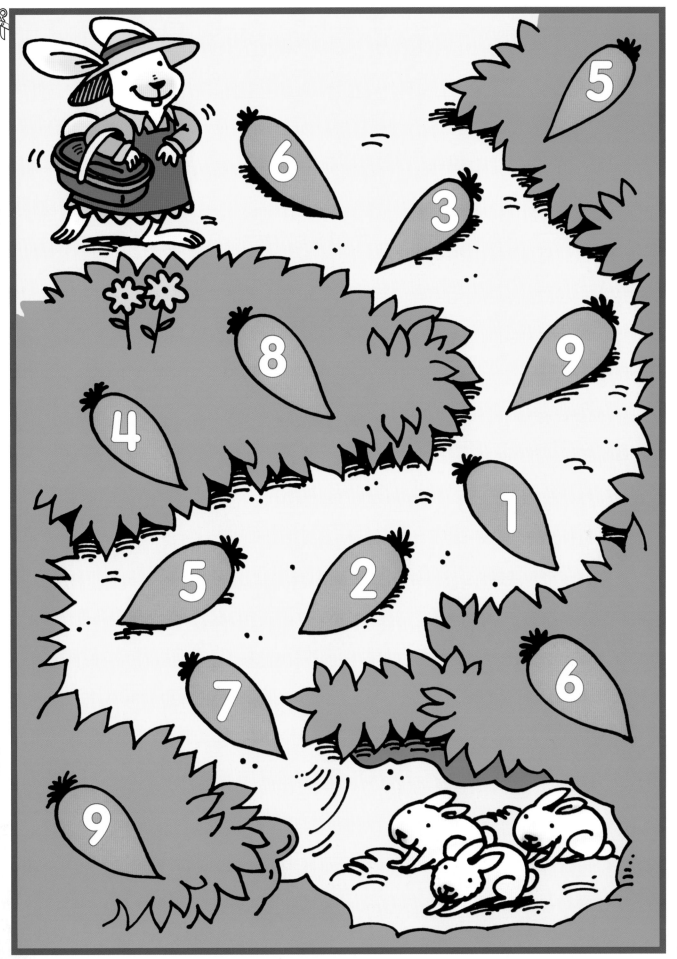

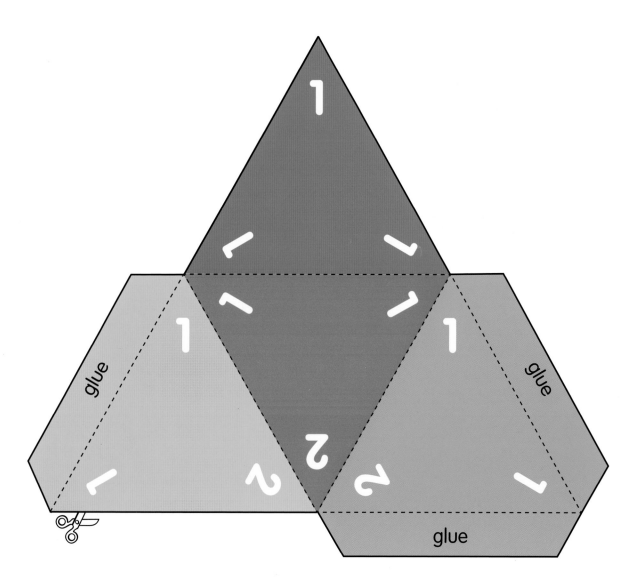

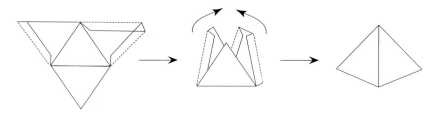

Assemble the pyramid by folding as shown. Glue closed.

Alien-O!

PLAYERS: 2

 SKILL
This game gives children practice in addition and subtraction facts.

INTRODUCTION

Show children one game card at a time. Ask them to read the math fact carefully to see whether they need to add or subtract. Then have them give the answer. After reviewing all of the cards, remind children that they should look carefully at the sign used in the problems to check that they are using the correct function to come up with their answers.

ASSEMBLING THE GAME

1. Remove pages 133–143 from the book along the perforated lines. Cut out the file-folder label and pocket on page 133. Glue the label onto the file-folder tab. Tape the sides and bottom of the pocket to the front of the folder.

2. Cut out the directions, answer key, and game cards on pages 135, 137, and139. When the game is not in use, store these items in the pocket on the front of the folder.

3. Cut out the two game boards on pages 141 and 143 and glue them to the inside of the folder.

EXTENDING THE GAME

Copy the game boards and cut out each square. Also, copy and cut out the game cards. Glue each cutout to an index card. Invite children to match each fact card to a matching answer card. Or pair up the fact and answer cards. Then choose 12 pairs of cards for children to use to play Memory. To play, children turn over two cards at a time to try to find matches.

Alien-O!

GET READY TO PLAY

- Each player chooses a game board.
- Shuffle the game cards. Pass out 20 cards to each player.
- Players stack their cards facedown.

TO PLAY

1 Both players take the top card from their stack at the same time.

2 Solve the math fact on your card. Is the answer on your game board?
- If so, put the card on the match.
- If not, put the card at the bottom of the other player's stack.

3 After each turn, check the answer key. Is your answer correct? If not, take the card back.

4 Players keep taking the top card at the same time and looking for matches. Try to cover four boxes in a row—going across, down, or diagonally. The first player to do this calls out "Alien-O!" That player wins the game.

PLAYING TIP

Play the game another way: Try to cover all of your boxes.
The first player to do this wins the game.

Alien-O!

ANSWER KEY

1 + 2 = 3	5 + 5 = 10	7 + 9 = 16	6 − 4 = 2	10 − 8 = 2	14 − 5 = 9
2 + 3 = 5	5 + 9 = 14	8 + 1 = 9	7 − 6 = 1	11 − 3 = 8	15 − 8 = 7
2 + 5 = 7	6 + 4 = 10	8 + 7 = 15	7 − 3 = 4	11− 5 = 6	16 − 7 = 9
3 + 8 = 11	6 + 7 = 13	9 + 6 = 15	8 − 5 = 3	12 − 6 = 6	17 − 9 = 8
3 + 9 =12	6 + 8 = 14	9 + 8 = 17	9 − 4 = 5	12 − 7 = 5	18 − 9 = 9
4 + 6 = 10	7 + 4 = 11	9 + 9 = 18	9 − 8 = 1	13 − 5 = 8	
4 + 8 = 12	7 + 6 = 13	5 − 1 = 4	10 − 7 = 3	13 − 6 = 7	

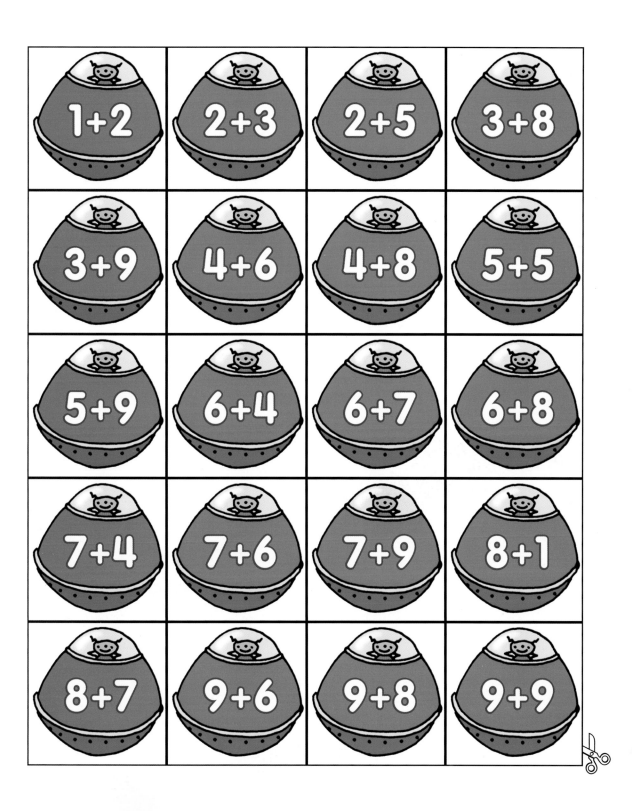

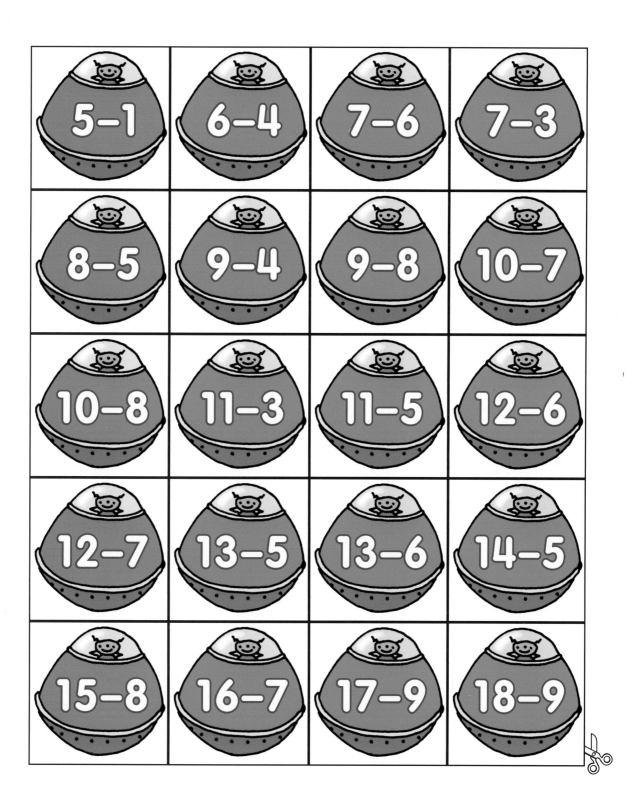